D1796127

Checking Up

# Checking Up

*How the Coalition's plans to cut back
on criminal records checks have been defeated*

Josie Appleton

Civitas: Institute for the Study of Civil Society
London

First Published October 2014

© Civitas 2014
55 Tufton Street
London SW1P 3QL

email: books@civitas.org.uk

All rights reserved

ISBN: 978-1-906837-66-2

Independence: Civitas: Institute for the Study of Civil
Society is a registered educational charity (No. 1085494)
and a company limited by guarantee (No. 04023541).
Civitas is financed from a variety of private sources to
avoid over-reliance on any single or small group
of donors.

All publications are independently refereed. All the
Institute's publications seek to further its objective of
promoting the advancement of learning. The views
expressed are those of the authors, not of the Institute.

Typeset by
Kevin Dodd

Printed in Great Britain by
Berforts Group Ltd
Stevenage, SGI 2BH

# *Contents*

# *Author*

Josie Appleton is director of the Manifesto Club civil liberties group, and has led the group's work on the vetting and barring scheme since the passing of the Safeguarding Vulnerable Groups Act in 2006. She has written over a dozen reports about the growth of child protection measures which have featured widely in print and broadcast media, from The Times to Panorama. She has also written influential reports on issues such as on-the-spot fines, anti-social behaviour powers, the regulation of leafleting, and restrictions in public spaces. Her research interest is to examine the new forms taken by contemporary state regulation and the effect of regulation on the operation of civic life.

# *Acknowledgements*

I would like to thank those who agreed to be interviewed for this report, including Professor Eileen Munro, Shaun Joynson, Julie Spence, Chris Stacey and Carrie Herbert. I would particularly like to thank Mervyn Barrett for sharing his decades of experience of the development of criminal records checks and for loaning policy documents from his collection. Thanks are also due to the two anonymous referees whose comments on an earlier draft of this report were extremely helpful.

# *Executive summary*

- In June 2010, the Coalition government promised to 'scale back' criminal records checks to 'common-sense proportions'. This came in the wake of a public debate led by children's authors and others, who claimed that mass vetting was unnecessary and was having a negative effect on trust and the relations between the generations. The government limited the number of people who should be vetted for working or volunteering with children, and predicted that its reforms would lead to a halving of criminal records checks, from around 4 million to 1.7 million.

- This has not happened. In 2013-14, there were in fact 3,948,793 criminal records checks, 843,498 of which were on volunteers. In fact, far from being scaled back, in certain ways the vetting system appears to have become more complicated, expansive and expensive. There are now no fewer than 23 different criminal records checks, each of which must be sought for different roles (such as volunteer/non-volunteer, working with children/ vulnerable adults). In 2013-14, the cost to society of criminal records checks was £211.6 million, more than when the government announced its reforms four years ago.

- The vetting system has continued to grow. The vetting and barring system now involves 730 direct employees of the Disclosure and Barring Service (DBS), hundreds of employees of police forces, workers from 3,688 registered bodies who submit checks, and 300 employees from the private company Tata Consultancy Services Ltd, as well as unpaid contributions from thousands of volunteers and representatives of community groups. The new system of instant online checks will mean that vetting has the potential to be extended still further into everyday life, and to become more of a routine request than it is at present.

- Why have the reforms failed? First, the argument of this report is that, in spite of good intentions, the Coalition government left intact too many elements of the previous vetting and barring system. In retrospect, the period since the reforms appears as a continuation rather than as a systemic shift. Second, vetting is encouraged by state agencies, such as local authorities and regulators, who demand checks even beyond current guidance. Finally, there is the role played by the private interests of the DBS and private umbrella bodies, who subsist from the income of checks and so have little interest in reducing or limiting unnecessary vetting.

- This report argues that the current scale of investment in vetting is out of proportion to its positive effects. Since 2002, criminal records checks have cost society two billion pounds, yet there has never been any significant research showing the effectiveness of mass vetting in child protection terms. The only major government research, in the early 1990s, concluded that mass vetting was of limited use and had potentially negative effects; this research recommended the limitation of vetting to a small number of posts. As former chief constable Julie Spence observes in this report, many police forces spend more time on vetting than on investigating child abuse accusations, or monitoring convicted child abusers upon release. That is, they spend more time and money monitoring a very large low-risk group – the general population – than the much smaller high-risk group of known or suspected offenders.

- At base, this report questions the central tenet of the British vetting and barring system over the past decade. This was an attempt to develop a central state vetting system for all those who come into relationships with children in the public sphere of a particular frequency or intensity (the legal category known as 'regulated activity'). The category of regulated activity is based on the notion that a certain degree of contact between adults and children provides an opportunity to develop 'a relationship of trust', which in turn presents an opportunity for abuse.

- This report identifies a number of problems with the notion of regulated activity. First, it is mistrustful and undermining of relationships between adults and children: it views abuse, not as a minority and criminal activity, but as the outcome of a certain frequency of contact. Second, the notion of 'regulated activity' is inherently confusing: civil servants have spent many months over the past decade trying to decide the exact number and type of meeting with children which provides an 'opportunity for trust', producing surreal reasoning and numerous shifts in policy. Finally, 'regulated activity' places undue faith in official checks as the provider of security, with the criminal records check fast becoming an index of trustworthiness.

- In conclusion, the report calls for a fundamental review of the vetting and barring system, a critical consideration of its costs and benefits. Unfortunately, there is little recent substantial academic or policy research into the operations or effectiveness of the vetting and barring system. Given that the Coalition's reforms have not resolved the problems with the vetting system, there is a need to go back to the drawing board, and to ask if criminal records checks are the best manner in which to be spending £200 million a year.

# Introduction:
## The failure of vetting reforms

In June 2010, the Coalition government promised to 'scale back' criminal records checks to 'common-sense proportions'.[1]

At this point, criminal records checks had become routine for anyone involved in their communities, including bell-ringers in churches, volunteer football coaches, a mother helping out at her daughter's nursery or a grandparent listening to reading in school. Vetting would be taken to a new level by plans for a vetting database contained in the Safeguarding Vulnerable Groups Act 2006, under which all adults who worked or volunteered with children would be placed on a database and subject to constant criminal records vetting.

Yet there was a growing criticism that vetting had escalated beyond sensible or necessary levels. There was also a widely expressed sentiment that over-cautious child protection checks were having some negative effects, undermining trust between the generations, and creating barriers to community activity such as putting off volunteers.

The debate came to a head when several high-profile children's authors refused to be vetted or registered on a database for their work in schools. In the view of author Philip Pullman, the 'insulting' request for checks treated everyone as potential paedophiles: 'It assumes that the default position of one human being to another is predatory rather than kindness… the basic mode is not of trust but suspicion'.[2] The Civitas report *Licensed to Hug*, by

Frank Furedi and Jennie Bristow, argued that vetting was leading to a formalisation of relationships between the generations, eroding the ordinary ways in which adults helped and cared for children.

The Coalition government sought to respond to these concerns. Home Secretary Theresa May argued that mass vetting treated everyone as 'guilty until proven innocent'; it was time, she said, to begin 'to trust each other again'.[3] To this end, the government passed the Protection of Freedoms Act 2012, abolishing the vetting database and, it claimed, limiting vetting to only those in the 'most sensitive' positions. These changes were enacted in September 2012. In the wake of this, many assumed that a sensible balance had been struck and the problem of over-cautious vetting had now been solved. The government predicted that reforms would lead to 'a reduction of some 50 per cent in the number of... certificates being issued, dropping from about 3.7 million a year to something like 1.7 million'.[4]

Yet this has not happened. In fact, there were 3,948,793 criminal records checks in 2013-14[5] – a slight decline from a high point of 2010-11, but more than in 2008-9, and a far cry from the government's estimated 1.7 million. Checks are still routine for church welcomers, bell-ringers, people listening to reading in schools, as well as public sector workers such as tree surgeons or heating engineers who may 'come into contact' with children by virtue of working in a public place.

There have been certain changes. Most visibly, Criminal Records Bureau (CRB) checks are now known as Disclosure and Barring Service (DBS) checks. The plans for the vetting database were scrapped. But on the ground, many people working in community groups have failed to notice any significant reductions in red tape. A Scout volunteer summarised recently:

> The reforms have clearly not made anything better so far from where I stand. I'm organising an overnight camp for families to celebrate 50 years of scouting in our village, and have to undertake a DBS check on every single parent or over-18-year-old attending, even though I'm aware that many of them have been checked recently by other organisations in the village. The Scout Association has so far shown no sign of 'scaling back'…[6]

Similar accounts are received by the Manifesto Club on a regular basis, indicating that vetting continues to present a barrier for community events and voluntary organisations. There have been recent cases of school events being cancelled because the school was unable to get a sufficient number of DBS-checked parent volunteers; there are also accounts of clubs or events from which children are barred because the adults had not been vetted.

So why have the reforms failed? In part, it could be seen as the result of over-cautious policies by individual schools or other institutions – a 'better-safe-than-sorry' approach. However, there is also a fundamental issue of the tentative nature of the government's reforms. In spite of the government's intentions to inaugurate a new era of 'common sense', the reforms left intact the central structure of the vetting and barring system. Rather than effecting a substantial transformation, the reforms were like a façade, erected in front of the old system.

Therefore, although the Protection of Freedoms Act inaugurated a new definition of those who *must* be criminal records checked (the legal category known as 'regulated activity'), this was not greatly different from the old; furthermore, the guidance on the new definition is unclear and so likely to encourage an over-cautious approach. In addition, the reforms left in place the old definition of 'regulated activity', only now meaning those who are *eligible* for checks. So there are currently two different definitions: those who *must* be vetted before they can work with children; and those who *can* be vetted if the organisation chooses. This has meant, first, that there is in fact no tighter legal limit on checks than there was under the previous government; and second, that many organisations find the law confusing and so understandably resort to blanket criminal records checks as a default policy.

Vetting is also encouraged by state institutions such as local authorities, which continue to encourage or demand criminal records checks beyond the remit of the current law. FOI requests show that, in 2013-14, local authorities carried out 661,092 checks on volunteers including: parents helping out at the school disco; parent volunteers with the school 'walking bus'; volunteers who drive elderly people to the shops; and parents helping out on school trips or listening to children reading. Local authorities also carried out checks for a broad range of public sector jobs, including: 'tree surgeon', 'beauty therapy lecturer' and 'healthy lifestyles coordinator'.[7]

These statistics are reinforced by the account from one long-time volunteer, who reports that in the past few months he has been asked for criminal records checks from two London local authorities, in both cases for voluntary activities where the children's parents would be present (and so would be responsible for their children). When he challenged the requests he was told that the criminal records check was a 'requirement' without which he couldn't volunteer.[8]

In addition, there seems to be an essential conflict of interest between the Home Office goal of 'scaling back' vetting, and the fact that the DBS subsists from the income of checks and has an interest in checks continuing at a high level. The DBS is a non-departmental public body of the Home Office but is self-financing, and issues annual corporate reports forecasting the 'disclosure volumes' for the year ahead. This conflict of interest is indicated by the fact that, at the same point that the Home Office was forecasting a 50 percent drop in checks to 1.7 million, the DBS forecasted over four million checks for the year ahead. If criminal records checks did fall to 1.7 million, the DBS would be left seriously indebted.

The vetting and barring system has continued to grow. It now involves 730 direct employees of the DBS,[9] hundreds of employees of police forces, workers from 3,688 registered bodies,[10] and 300 employees from the private company Tata Consultancy Services, which works with the DBS, as well as the unpaid contributions from thousands of volunteers and representatives of community groups. Since 2002, criminal records checks have cost society two billion pounds.

From a social policy perspective, one has to ask whether results justify such a major investment of social resources. Indeed, one has to ask whether these resources could not be better spent elsewhere, to greater positive effect.

This report first reviews the history and rise of the vetting and barring system, before going on to question its efficacy.

# 1

# Regulating trust: A decade of vetting and barring policy

*A decade of vetting and barring policy*

Over the past decade, there have been several different bodies responsible for vetting – the Criminal Records Bureau, Independent Safeguarding Authority and the current Disclosure and Barring Service – which have been subject to name changes, mergers and abolitions. There have been several reviews and many changes of rules about exactly who should and should not be vetted.

The vetting and barring system was enacted in the Safeguarding Vulnerable Groups Act 2006 on the advice of the 2004 Bichard Report investigating Ian Huntley's murder of two schoolgirls in the village of Soham in 2002. At its outset, the vetting and barring scheme was supposed to affect 8.5 million people. This number then rose to 11.3 million; then, after policy changes, fell to nine million; and finally arrived at its current level of five million. However, these numbers are relatively hazy estimates: officials have never really known how many people fall within the category of those who must be vetted by law.

The Labour government's vetting and barring system was from the start a labyrinthine project of an intrinsically confusing nature. I have sat in several government roadshows where local authority workers and others struggled to understand the rules on exactly who should and who should not be vetted. The minister present was sometimes unable to answer audience questions and had to call upon a civil servant to explain whether or not a particular post would fall within the requirements of the Act. This uncertainty and continual re-education of people in the 'latest requirements' has continued to the present. The 2012 Independent Safeguarding Authority (ISA) annual report stated that the year had included work on 'new guidance, toolkits, roadshows – VB [vetting and barring] policy roadshow has been on the road for a decade now!'[11] Indeed it has: for a decade, the vetting organisation of the day has been travelling around the country telling people what they need to do to comply with the law, and who needs to be vetted. Then procedures change, which means more roadshows and more guidance.

However, what has been constant over this period, which marks out contemporary vetting policy as unusual both historically and in relation to other countries, is the assumption that *it is the role of the central state to vet those who come into relationships of particular intensity with children in the public sphere*. This category of relationships is defined as 'regulated activity', and the control of 'regulated activity' remains at the cornerstone of vetting policy. The idea of regulated activity is unprecedented, and unique when compared to the vetting regimes in other countries and to Britain in the past.

There has always been vetting of certain professions, such as teachers or lawyers; this vetting was often carried out by the professional bodies themselves and was part of establishing a person's fitness to practise a profession. There were also systems for monitoring child abusers and other offenders, such as probation systems or, more recently, the Sex Offenders' Register.

Yet 'regulated activity' is quite different: it is vetting as a default policy for all adults coming into contact with children through their work or volunteering. It is not regulating known offenders, or the professions, but people who came into a certain 'intensity' or 'frequency' of contact with children. The idea of regulated activity is a regulation of relationships between adults and children in the public sphere.

Under the vetting and barring scheme, for the first time, people helping out at a local club or group were expected to carry out a 'test' to see if they were 'engaging in regulated activity'. The 'test for regulated activity' was the frequency or length of a person's encounters with children. The policy assumption was that meetings of a certain frequency or in a particular context would mean that a person had an 'opportunity to develop a relationship of trust' with a child, which in turn would mean a potential opportunity to abuse that child. One 2009 policy document explained the logic: 'were the same person to teach children in a class every Saturday, or every fortnight, they would have the opportunity to develop a relationship of trust with their class and, therefore pose a greater risk of harm.'[12]

Therefore, frequent contact was seen as an opportunity to develop a relationship of trust, which in turn was seen as a 'risk of harm' or 'opportunity to abuse'. This policy approach is based on the notion that abuse is the potential outcome of a certain number of encounters, and that all adults in this position pose a potential risk to children. It also assumes that state vetting is the means in which this danger can be assuaged.

Policy advisers expended great effort in attempting to establish how many meetings with a child or children would be necessary in order that somebody had the potential to develop this 'relationship of trust'. Between the publication of the Bichard Report in 2004 and the abolition of the database in 2010 there were six years of policy wrangling, attempting to pin down the exact scope of those who should be subject to state vetting.

The first definition of 'regulated activity' was: caring for or instructing children, which occurred 'frequently', defined as once a month; or 'intensively', defined as three days at a time; or 'overnight', defined as occurring between 2am and 6am. It would also include all activity which occurred regularly or frequently in a series of defined institutions, including schools, children's homes, hospitals, nurseries, regardless of whether they were instructing or caring for children.

An increasing number of anomalies and questions presented themselves. Civil servants considered cases such as exercise or pottery classes where children come along: should the course leader be vetted? Should a taxi driver be vetted who occasionally drives children? Did it count if somebody gave a course every week to different children? How many months did an event have to occur for before it 'met the frequency test'?

The policy documents became longer, as officials considered more of these examples. One 149-page document expended several pages on the example of adult classes where children came along.[13] Officials decided that the course leader didn't have to be vetted if children just happened to come along – children were, in the jargon, 'merely incidental' to the class. However, as time goes on, and 'children start to attend on a regular basis independently in their own right and come to take an active role in the society, then their attendance is not incidental to that of adults', and the instructor or teacher would have to be vetted. If an activity were 'targeted at both adults and children' – for example, an aerobics class was advertised 'All ages welcome' – then the course leader would have to be checked, even if a very small number of children (or indeed, no children) came to the group.

These documents proposed unworldly standards, imagining people analysing their posters for any phrases welcoming children, or counting the number of their interactions with children, and informing the authorities at the appropriate time. For example, a taxi driver would have to be on the database once they had conveyed children the requisite number of times, meaning that taxi drivers would be expected to count the number of times they had driven children, and submit themselves for clearance once they reached the defined levels of 'frequently' or 'intensively'. Similarly, a volunteer cricket coach who helped out for a weekend would not have to be vetted, but if the training session went on another day then the club should realise that he had 'worked intensively with children' and submit him for vetting.

Over time, benchmarks were constantly reviewed and adjusted, with the Singleton Review under Labour in 2009, and the Protection of Freedoms Act in 2012. A series of exemptions were added over time, as officials realised the difficulty of regulating sectors such as Saturday jobs and foreign exchange visits.

*Table 1: Definition of 'Regulated Activity'*

| DATE | Meaning of 'Frequently' | Meaning of 'Intensively' | Exemptions from regulated activity | No. of people affected |
|------|-------------------------|--------------------------|-----------------------------------|------------------------|
| 2006 – Safeguarding Vulnerable Groups Act | Once a month | Three days at a time; or overnight (2am-6am) | Employment of children, e.g. Saturday jobs; activity with children 'merely incidental' to adults, e.g. bus driver | Estimates started at 8.5 million (2006); rose to 10 and then 11.3 million |
| December 2009: Singleton review[14] | Once a week | Four days at a time; or overnight | People who work with different children; foreign exchange visits | 9 Million |
| 2012 – Protection of Freedoms Act[15] | Once a week | Four or more days at a time; or overnight | Under-16s; providers of occasional and temporary services; volunteers supervised by vetted professionals; legal advice | 5 million |

## Current policy

The current government seeks to distinguish its own vetting policy sharply from that of the previous government. One guidance document said that

11

previous vetting policy had created 'public confusion, a fearful workforce and a dysfunctional culture of mistrust between children and adults. This Government is taking a different approach.'[16] And yet the new policy continues in a remarkably similar vein to previous versions. The government's new definition of 'regulated activity' creates new exemptions, but it is not substantially different to the definition agreed in the Labour government's Singleton Review in December 2009 (the definitions of 'frequently' and 'intensively' are the same). The main change is a removal of 'supervised volunteers' from vetting requirements, but it is difficult to see how this change would account for a three million drop in the numbers of people who must be vetted.

Current policy is also founded on the idea that 'contact' between adults and children is a precursor to potential abuse and should therefore be regulated. One policy document justifies the regulation of all 'overnight' activity on the basis that it provides 'opportunity for face-to-face contact with children'; another says that a person must be vetted if their work in schools 'gives the person the opportunity, in their work, to have contact with children'.[17]

The new definition of regulated activity is potentially more complicated and places a greater onus on organisations to engage in a detailed process of considering whether or not a particular role falls within the definition of regulated activity. For example, the guidance document on the meaning of 'supervised volunteers' – those who are exempted from obligatory vetting – defines supervision as: 'reasonable in all the circumstances to ensure the protection of children'.[18]

The document suggests that a head teacher should engage in detailed consideration of each volunteering role in order to discover whether a person should be vetted. In each case, 'organisations should consider the following factors: ages of the children, including whether their ages differ widely; number of children that the individual is working with; whether or not other workers are helping to look after the children; the nature of the individual's work (or, in a specified place such as a school, the individual's opportunity for contact with children); how vulnerable the children are (the more they are, the more an organisation might opt for workers to be in regulated activity); how many workers would be supervised by each supervising worker.'

The guidance document includes a model scenario:

> Mr Jones, a new volunteer, helps children with reading at a local school for two mornings a week. Mr Jones is generally based in the classroom, in sight of the teacher. Sometimes Mr Jones takes some of the children to a separate room to listen to them reading, where Mr Jones is supervised by a paid classroom assistant, who is in that room most of the time. The teacher and classroom assistant are in regulated activity. The head teacher decides whether their supervision is such that Mr Jones is not in regulated activity.

Such model scenarios are frequently found in vetting policy documents. Only in this case there is no 'answer' given: the school is expected to find the correct answer itself, asking in the case of each volunteer whether the supervision is 'reasonable in all the circumstances to ensure the protection of children', and keeping documents to justify the decisions they have made in the case of each specific volunteer.

There appears to be little sense of the fact that it would be unrealistic for a head teacher to examine the exact nature of each volunteer's contact with children, or the exact nature of a teacher's supervision, since these things would vary from case to case and week to week, depending on a host of factors that affect schedules in a busy school. The request that head teachers undertake this exercise is especially unreasonable, given that many of these volunteers would be parents or grandparents of children at the school and already known to teachers and other children.

It is little surprise that there is substantial confusion about the new laws on vetting, and many remain unsure about who should and should not be vetted. Volunteering England produced a flow chart seeking to outline the new definition of 'regulated activity' for voluntary groups, but in spite of studying the law closely, it could only say that a particular role 'appears to be' or 'appears not to be' within the new definition 'regulated activity'.[19]

## *The impact of vetting policy on trust*

In spite of the unworldly and confusing nature of vetting policy, over the years it has filtered into people's consciousness and affected the way in which they see their relationships with children.

It is striking to note how the most respectable of adults will often use the terms such as 'access' and 'contact' to describe their encounters with children. On one online discussion board, for example, mothers helping out at their children's schools discussed the circumstances in which they require a criminal records check. They used the same phrases found in policy documents: they said that they need checks when they have 'contact' or a 'chance of "one-on-one" contact', 'unsupervised access', or when they have direct and very private 'access' such as helping out on 'toilet duty' or changing after swimming.[20]

Here we see how a group of mothers, who are the least likely child abusers in the world, nonetheless discuss and experience their interactions with children in the public sphere as risky and subject to formal regulation. 'Toilet duty' – one of the primary needs of very young children, a commonplace for mothers – is transformed into a high-risk activity which requires special clearance.

One mother recounted how 'a list was made of parents who had been CRB checked and they were the only ones who were able to help with toilet duty'.[21] There have also been several accounts of volunteers made to wear different coloured t-shirts according to whether or not they had been checked, and only those who had been 'enhanced checked' could take children to the toilet.[22] Such colour coding is a visual demonstration of the logic at play: every adult is marked by their degree of clearance, which equates to degree of trustworthiness, and permission for a certain degree of contact with children.

This shows also how attempts to limit vetting to those who have particular kinds of 'access' or 'contact' can actually intensify the mistrustful message behind vetting policy. A tighter definition of 'regulated activity' can mean a more conscious organisation and segregation of informal relationships along the lines of degree of 'contact' and 'access', and the corresponding degree of security clearance required.

# 2

# Criminal records checks – a 'safe adult' card

*The rise of the criminal records check*

Twenty years ago, the criminal records check was a relatively rare event, limited to certain professions. Before someone became a teacher, lawyer or accountant, a police check would often be carried out to check that there was no good reason why they should not join this profession. The check on criminal records was, along with references, a manner in which professions established their boundaries and made decisions about who was fit to practise.

In addition to the police check, for teachers there was also a check on a list of individuals barred from working with children, known as List 99, which was held by the Department of Education.

The transformation of criminal records checks started to occur at the end of the 1990s. When criminal records checks were first introduced for purposes of child protection in 1986, it was estimated that 100,000 would be conducted annually. In the event, by 1988, 540,000 were conducted, rising to 607,000 in 1995.[23]

A significant shift came in 1999, when the Protection of Children Act 1999 gave access to barred lists to a new range of organisations (such as those providing childcare) and also encouraged voluntary organisations such as the Scouts to join the system.[24] The 1997 Police Act had provided for the creation of an independent, fee-charging body for the processing of criminal records: this occurred in 2002, and the newly formed Criminal Records Bureau took over vetting from police forces.

After this point, CRB checks started to multiply year on year, and by 2009 had surpassed four million, a level at which they have remained ever since. This eight-fold increase in criminal records vetting since the 1990s represents a fundamental transformation in the role of these checks.

*Table 2: Criminal records checks, 2002-2014\**

| Year | Enhanced CRB checks | Standard CRB checks | Checks on Volunteers | Total CRBs Issued |
|---|---|---|---|---|
| 2002/3 | 1,258,656 | 178,327 | 210,571 | 1,436,983 |
| 2003/4 | 2,002,161 | 285,275 | 414,816 | 2,287,436 |
| 2004/5 | 2,157,637 | 275,292 | 499,354 | 2,432,929 |
| 2005/6 | 2,462,404 | 313,959 | 574,856 | 2,776,363 |
| 2006/7 | 2,948,794 | 329,234 | 668,715 | 3,278,028 |
| 2007/8 | 3,028,793 | 294,607 | 673,561 | 3,323,400 |
| 2008/9 | 3,459,992 | 396,586 | 742,556 | 3,856,578 |
| 2009/10 | 4,007,147 | 294,154 | 902,102 | 4,301,301 |
| 2010/11 | 4,125,289 | 187,243 | 962,528 | 4,312,532 |
| 2011/12 | 3,755,885 | 256,952 | 922,141 | 4,012,837 |
| 2012/13 | 3,801,064 | 265,541 | 887,914 | 4,066,605 |
| 2013/14† | – | – | 843,498 | 3,948,793 |

*Data for 2002-2011 from FOI response, 17 April 2012; data for 2012-13 from FOI response, 26 February 2014
†2013-14 data from DBS FOI response, 12 May 2014

The shift can be summarised as follows. Criminal records checks started as a recruitment tool for certain professions, based on concern with a variety of offences. Now they have transformed into an all-purpose 'safe adult' card, for all those who have contact with children or 'vulnerable adults' in the public sphere.

Those checked were now from a much wider range of

jobs, such as ski instructors or sports coaches, who work with children but were not child professionals. There were also checks on those who could have contact with children through their work. Local authorities started to ask for checks on workers such as people selling burgers from vans, tree surgeons or swimming pool managers – people who, because their job involves interacting with members of the public, or just being in a public place, have the 'possibility' of 'contact with children'.

Most significantly, there was also a move of criminal records checks into the voluntary sector and informal sphere of civil society. The proportion of volunteers being checked rose from 14 per cent of total checks in 2002 to 23 per cent in 2011, a rise in number from 210,571 to 922,141. At this point, volunteers helping out at a Saturday cricket club became subject to the same level of clearance as those in child professions such as children's care homes, and required a greater level of clearance than is required for sellers of explosives.[25]

Over time, the criminal record check raised unrealistic expectations. Rather than just being seen as a specific tool – a search of the police national computer and barred lists – the criminal records check started to be seen as a vouchsafe indicator that a person could be trusted. To have a 'clean CRB' increasingly meant: 'I am a responsible person and can be trusted'. On the same basis, an unchecked person was often viewed as inherently suspicious; those waiting for their check to come through would be barred from undertaking their duties or subject to special restrictive measures until the certificate arrived.

Moreover, increasingly it was not enough for

someone to be checked once: people had to be checked constantly, by every new voluntary organisation or institution with which they worked. In 2006, the CRB stopped accepting 'portability requests', which release the results of a past CRB, 'because of the risk factors involved'. Hence, a person would need one check for the local cricket team, one for being a teacher, another for being a Scout, with each institution carrying its own check as part of its recruitment process.

Different institutions established their own rules on the period after which a fresh check must be sought: for some this was a year, for others two or three years. Another rule in many schools (derived from government guidance 'Safeguarding Children and Safer Recruitment',[26] which is still in force) was that if a school volunteer was absent for a period of three months they would have to undergo a new check. As one parent reported in autumn 2012:

> My children are at the local primary school and I help out there occasionally, usually by helping out on school trips. I have been advised that unless I help out at least every three months I would need another CRB check. That is, for parents that have been CRB checked, but have not been in contact with children in school time during the previous three months, then the school are asking for another CRB check. I already have three enhanced CRB checks in my professional role in the local hospital, in primary care and as a volunteer. The head teacher took advice from our county council, who said that as long as the helper was not alone with the child then this was sometimes acceptable but that they would not advise it. I help out on school trips which occur two to three times a year and I understand that I would require a new CRB check each time as the period between trips is usually longer than three months. Saying that, the Head Teacher did allow me on the trip this time as long as I did not accompany any children into the toilets.[27]

It is easy to see how this mentality chimed with the idea of a vetting database, with those on it being constantly checked, since it is only by constant searching of one's files that one could be declared 'eligible to work with children'. The database would have centralised and simplified this culture of constant checking.

## DBS checks today

The notion that underpinned the database project – that people need to be constantly checked in order to be declared safe – is still with us, but has found different expressions in more fragmented, costly and confusing avenues, such as in repeat criminal records checks, or in the new 'update service'.

The new portability element to DBS checks (called the 'update service') is intended to ease red tape and avoid the hassle of repeat checks. The update service involves many of the same elements of the vetting database but is in certain ways more cumbersome and fragmented. It works as follows. A person subscribed to the 'update service' will have the barred list and criminal records on the police national computer searched every week; local police information will be searched every nine months. If there is 'new information', both they and their voluntary organisation or employer will be told that the check is 'no longer current', and they will have to apply for a new check to see this 'new information'.[28] The update service requires a continual issuing of DBS checks, as well as the annual payment of a £13 fee (although there is no service fee for volunteers). For an employed person, this would mean a first payment of around £77,[29] then the annual subscription, as opposed to the one-off payment of £64 that would have been required for registration on the vetting database. While the vetting database would have recorded simply that a person was 'cleared to work with children', without releasing criminal records information, the 'update service' is a system for continually checking the validity of particular criminal records certificates, which will continue to be issued in full.

This is complicated by the fact that there are now many different kinds of DBS check, each of which relates to a particular kind of working position. First, checks are of different security levels: a 'standard' check involves a search of the police national computer, an 'enhanced' check additionally involves a search of local police files. An enhanced check can be requested for work that falls under the old definition of 'regulated activity', the standard check for a broader range of positions, and the barred list check can only be requested for jobs falling under the new definition of 'regulated activity'.[30] In June 2013, the DBS created new 'workforce' categories, so every check must additionally specify if it is for the 'child', 'adult' or 'other' workforce.[31]

Therefore, a check could be 'enhanced for children's workforce with a barred list check'; or 'enhanced for adult's workforce without barred list check', or 'standard for adult workforce'. These different variables for the types of checks leads to no fewer than 11 different possible DBS checks:

*Table 3: Categories of criminal records checks*

|  | Children's barred list check | Adults' barred list | Adults' and children's barred lists | No barred list |
|---|---|---|---|---|
| Standard – adult workforce |  |  |  | ✗ |
| Standard – child workforce |  |  |  | ✗ |
| Standard – other |  |  |  | ✗ |
| Standard – adult and child |  |  |  | ✗ |
| Enhanced – adult |  | ✗ |  | ✗ |
| Enhanced – child | ✗ |  |  | ✗ |
| Enhanced – adult and child |  |  | ✗ | ✗ |
| Enhanced – other |  |  |  | ✗ |

Each of these can be a volunteer or non-volunteer position, meaning a total of 22 different checks. There is also an 'adults first' check – a check of the adults barred list while waiting for a check to come through – which takes the total number of checks to 23.

Anybody subscribed to the update service will still be required to seek repeat DBS checks for different roles, and even to sign up to different 'update services' for their different roles. So, for example, a DBS certificate for a paid position cannot be added to an 'update service' set up for a voluntary position: you would need to set up two different update services. You also need different checks for different 'workforces': so, if you have a check for helping out at the local football team, and then you volunteer to drive elderly people to the shops, you would need a separate check (the first is the 'children's workforce', the second is the 'adults' workforce').

Additionally, not all organisations will accept the 'update service', and so will request new criminal records checks anyway.[32] All this means that somebody could be paying an annual subscription for the update service – they could even have two accounts – and yet still be reapplying for one of 23 different criminal records checks on a relatively regular basis.

In summary, the new system has maintained the culture of constant checking that was inherent in the vetting database, yet at greater complication and cost.

Finally, the new update service removes many of the limitations that rightfully exist around requests to view criminal records. With the update service, a request to see your criminal record can be carried out online and is called a 'status check': the employer merely enters the code of a criminal records certificate, and ticks a box to say that he or she has the consent of the person. This potentially further expands the role of the criminal records check, making it more like an identity card which one is expected to hold and show upon request, rather than a secure document which must be requested each time, subject to specified limitations.

### The cost of vetting and barring

The trend over time has been a growing cost for the vetting and barring system, as the system has become increasingly expansive, complicated and subject to constant changes. The costs of the vetting and barring scheme can be broken down into two elements: criminal records checks costs and system costs.

#### (i) The costs of criminal records checks

The cost of criminal records checks can be broken down into the fees charged for checks, which are not payable by volunteers; and the approximately £20 administration fee which applies to all checks, including volunteers. (The DBS fee for volunteers' checks is borne by the fee-paying checks).

The table below shows that the total cost of criminal records checks has increased by 500 per cent since 2002. It is striking that the cost of checks has continued to rise since 2010, when the Coalition reforms were announced; and that the most expensive year yet was 2012-13, the year following the enacting of the Protection of Freedoms Act. In total, checks have cost nearly two billion pounds since 2002.

*Table 4: Cost of criminal records checks, 2002-2014*

| Year | Checks on Volunteers | Total CRBs Issued | Fees paid to CRB/DBS (£million)* | Admin costs (£million)† | Total cost (£million) |
|---|---|---|---|---|---|
| 2002/3 | 210,571 | 1,436,983 | 14.712 | 28.74 | 43.45 |
| 2003/4 | 414,816 | 2,287,436 | 50.175 | 45.75 | 95.93 |
| 2004/5 | 499,354 | 2,432,929 | 62.711 | 48.66 | 111.37 |
| 2005/6 | 574,856 | 2,776,363 | 75.496 | 55.53 | 131.03 |
| 2006/7 | 668,715 | 3,278,028 | 91.65 | 65.56 | 157.21 |
| 2007/8 | 673,561 | 3,323,400 | 96.311 | 66.47 | 162.78 |
| 2008/9 | 742,556 | 3,856,578 | 112.62 | 77.13 | 189.75 |
| 2009/10 | 902,102 | 4,301,301 | 124.15 | 86.03 | 210.18 |
| 2010/11 | 962,528 | 4,312,532 | 116.48 | 86.25 | 202.73 |
| 2011/12 | 922,141 | 4,012,837 | 131.55 | 80.26 | 211.81 |
| 2012/13 | 887,914 | 4,066,605 | 133.79 | 81.33 | 215.12 |
| 2013/14‡ | 843,498 | 3,948,793 | 132.633 | 78.97 | 211.60 |
| **TOTAL** | **8,302,612** | **40,033,785** | **1,142.28** | **800.68** | **1,942.96** |

*Data from CRB FOI response, 17 April 2012; and DBS FOI response, 12 May 2014
†Calculated using average administration cost of £20 per check
‡2013-14 data from DBS FOI response, 12 May 2014

Over this period, the cost of an enhanced criminal record check has increased from £12 to £44. This increase was partly in order to fund the increasingly large and complex vetting and barring system.

*Table 5: Cost of standard and enhanced checks, 2002-2011\**

|  | 22 Mar 2002 | 1 Jul 2003 | 1 Apr 2004 | 1 Apr 2005 | 1 Apr 2006 | 1 Apr 2007 | 1 Apr 2008 | 1 Apr 2009 | 1 Oct 2009 | 6 Apr 2011 |
|---|---|---|---|---|---|---|---|---|---|---|
| Enhanced check | £12 | £29 | £33 | £34 | £36 | £36 | £36 | £36 | £36 | £44 |
| Standard check | £12 | £24 | £28 | £29 | £31 | £31 | £31 | £31 | £26 | £26 |

*FOI response from the CRB, 17 April 2012

## (ii) Vetting and barring system costs

The frequent changes of vetting policy have also led to substantial system costs. At every stage, organisations have been created, abolished, merged; databases designed and then abandoned. There is no central record of these system costs, but indications can be obtained from several different sources.

*Table 6: System costs of criminal record checks*

| Item | Date | Cost (£000s) | Source |
|---|---|---|---|
| Disclosure and Barring Programme (DBP) | 2012-13 | 5,270 | Home Office FOI response, 21 June 2013 |
| ISA annual grant in aid, £10 million a year for 4.5 years | 2008-2012 | 45,000 | ISA annual reports |
| Vetting and Barring Scheme set-up costs |  | 84,000 | Home Office announcement, 1 April 2008 |

What is not recorded is the time and effort spent by organisations – many in the public or voluntary sector – attending vetting and barring roadshows, designing and then re-designing procedures to comply with the latest guidance.

## Where does the money go?

It is worth noting that the cost of the vetting and barring system is disproportionately borne by the public and voluntary sectors, and the profit is disproportionately enjoyed by a variety of private companies.

The largest portion (around 40 per cent) of income from criminal records checks is spent on private sector contractors, formerly Capita, and now Tata Consultancy Services Ltd (which won the eight-year, £350 million contract with the DBS[33] and will employ 300 people at an office in Liverpool).[34]

In addition, 15 of the top 20 processors of criminal records checks are private companies. In 2012-13, these private umbrella companies together processed 1,047,145 checks,[35] meaning an income of some £20 million.[36]

Indeed, the DBS itself is in some ways a private company within the state, since it is financially independent and relies on the income for checks. The DBS uses financial language and presents its work as a business, predicting in its most recent 'corporate plan' that: 'Our forecast for disclosure volumes for 1 April 2013 to 31 March 2014 are 4.07 million, of which approximately 3.1 million are expected to be from paying customers.'[37]

# 3

# Do criminal records checks work?

*The 'unsuitable people' claim*

The primary claim for the efficacy of criminal records checks is the DBS's assertion that 'At least 150,000 unsuitable individuals have been prevented from working with children and vulnerable groups as a direct result of a DBS check' since 2002.[38] This statistic is obtained from an annual survey of around 300 'registered bodies' (bodies which process criminal records checks) carried out by Mori on behalf of the CRB since 2002. If we examine this research, we must first note Mori's warnings that this figure is a 'very cautious extrapolation', which is based on interviewees' memory of the numbers of people from whom they have withdrawn job offers as a result of criminal records checks. More substantially, the detail of this research shows:

1.  These 150,000 'unsuitable individuals' have been denied jobs for offences other than child sex offences. Indeed, not one Mori report includes a statistic for the number of people denied jobs on the basis of child sex offences. The most common offences for which people are denied jobs are: theft, violence, drugs offences, driving offences, fraud/dishonesty.[39]

2.  A substantial number of individuals have lost jobs, not because of convictions, but because of information on local police files. In the 2012 Mori report, 37 per cent of withdrawn job offers were

because of information on local police files, which by definition had not been proven in a court of law.

Therefore, the DBS appears to be claiming that checks are keeping tens of thousands of child sex offenders away from children. What the survey actually finds is that: *thousands of people a year are losing jobs for convictions other than child sex offences, or on the basis of unproven local police information.*

The reports consistently find that the largest category of withdrawn job offers is in the care sector. Therefore, the average profile of one of these 150,000 individuals would be something like: a woman denied a position in an elderly care home because of a conviction or caution for shoplifting in her youth. One lady who worked in the care sector observed that this may be because 'young women and young mothers apply to work in the care sector and these are often the kind of women who have minor convictions such as shoplifting, violence (from poor relationships) or drug possession'.[40]

### Other research on the effectiveness of CRBs

Surprisingly, given the investment of resources in criminal checks, there has been no recent substantial research testing their effectiveness or investigating alternative mechanisms. Other research into the effectiveness of vetting was carried out in the early 1990s, at a time when the government was considering an expansion and restructuring of the police check system.

In 1989 the Home Office set up pilot schemes to test the use of criminal records checks in the voluntary sector. The independent report on these findings is a rare example of substantial research into the effectiveness and results of checks in a particular sector.[41]

The study came to the conclusion that criminal records checks were of 'minimal relevance' to child protection: 'the protective value of criminal records checks is doubtful', it said, and they provided a 'very limited and inadequate device for detecting proven abusers'. It concluded this on the basis that the majority of positive checks are for offences other than child abuse, and that many of those who pose a risk to children do not have a formal criminal record. The review also found that 'there is no evidence that known sexual offenders are targeting voluntary organisations in order to gain access to children'.[42] The report concluded that the vast majority of positive checks have 'no relevance to the safety of children'.

Indeed, the report observed a 'danger' that vetting gives rise to a 'false sense of security'. It noted that the attraction of criminal records checks was in part driven by organisations' desire to 'project a responsible and caring image', and in this sense 'the safety of the child often appears to be confused with the safety of the organisation'. The study noted that some organisations had 'an almost magical belief that a criminal records check makes an unsafe situation safe', and that organisations were using checks as a shortcut to dealing with situations of inadequate supervision or management.[43]

The report found that the average cost to a voluntary organisation was £15.50 per check; it also noted that vetting jarred with the 'ad hoc and informal' nature of many voluntary organisations.[44] In summary, it said that the consequence of vetting could be perverse, in that 'non-threatening individuals are barred from access to children while dangerous but hidden offenders are given positions of trust'. It recommended a restriction of vetting, and suggested a greater emphasis on supervision and vigilance within organisations as a more effective strategy.

These views were echoed in a Home Office consultation document in 1993,[45] which said that criminal records checks could have a deterrent effect and 'provide some reassurance to the public', but also noted many disadvantages, including: that many of the most disturbing cases of child sex abuse involved 'people with no convictions'; that checks are 'poorly targeted' towards the lower risk groups (it cites the fact that 98 per cent of sex offenders are male, but 68 per cent of those checked by voluntary organisations were female, meaning that the majority of checks are carried out on those who are extremely unlikely to offend sexually).[46] It also noted that checks 'can lead to complacency and a misguided assumption by employers and managers that their staff are "safe"'.[47] The consultation recommended the establishing of an independent, fee-charging body for the processing of checks – not because of the policy value of vetting, but primarily because the 'unmet demand' for checks was outstretching police capacity ('despite their deficiencies police checks have increasingly acquired the status of a "seal of approval" for child care workers'[48]). It was thought that fees and a legislative framework would limit the expansion of criminal records checks.

Because the criminal records check has become an index of trust, it is sometimes forgotten that it is just a search of a database, with all the ensuing limitations. Standard and enhanced checks involve a search of the Police National Computer (PNC) for non-expired cautions and convictions, and enhanced checks additionally involve a search of local police files. This is a rough tool, and there is a degree of uncertainty as to what will return on a check. As Christopher Stacey of Unlock points out: 'around 40 per cent of UK court convictions are not entered on to the PNC, since they are not recordable offences; and many convictions up to the mid-90s are also not registered on the PNC'.[49] At the same time, very minor or unproven information can be released through local police files. The release of local police information can be erratic, depending on the judgement of the police officer processing the check. Unlock therefore often finds it difficult to advise people whether or not a particular incident would return on a criminal records check, particularly given that individuals cannot get their own DBS check before applying for work.

However, some have argued that criminal records checks act as a deterrent, and that the existence of checks puts off convicted child abusers from applying for voluntary work with children. This claim was considered by the 1992 Home Office-funded pilot study, which concluded that: 'by its nature this is an assertion which is extremely difficult to test, and it appears to be uncorroborated by evidence of abuse in those very substantial areas of the voluntary sector which are not yet covered by vetting arrangements'.[50] Similarly, the claim appears to be uncorroborated by evidence from other European countries whose voluntary organisations are not regulated by a UK-style vetting system. (It is only some Australian states which share the UK's systematic legal obligation to vet volunteers who work with children, and the exemptions are much greater than our own.) This suggests that the deterrent effect is not very large; there is also a possibility of achieving the same end through different policy means (see Section 4, below).

## *The problems with barring policy*

The deficits of criminal records checks are increased by the problems of the new barring process, the second element of the vetting and barring scheme set up by New Labour in response to the Huntley case. These barring arrangements have been retained almost in their entirety by the present government.

The barring regime was run by the ISA, a role that has now been taken over by the DBS (which retains the ISA offices and many of its staff). This organisation now maintains the 'children's barred list' (a list of people barred from working with children) and the 'vulnerable adults barred list' (those barred from working with 'vulnerable adults' including elderly, homeless, disabled people, or adults receiving health care). These lists replace barred lists held by the departments for education and health.[51]

By law, those engaging in work which falls under the current definition of 'regulated activity' with children or vulnerable adults must carry out an enhanced criminal records check with the relevant barred list check. There are criminal offences of knowingly employing a barred person in regulated activity, and of a barred person seeking work in regulated activity.

However, there are reasons to doubt the effectiveness of the current barring system, in terms of its stated goal of identifying those individuals who pose a risk to children or others. In fact, there are indications that the barring system suffers from similar weaknesses to the vetting system, particularly an over-reliance on bureaucratic procedures.

A person can be placed on a barred list by one of two routes: either automatically, through an 'automatic bar'; or as a result of a 'discretionary bar' by ISA/DBS caseworkers, which is made through the 'barring decision-making process'.

First, the autobar. People are automatically barred from working with children or vulnerable adults upon receiving a conviction or caution for a 'relevant' offence' contained in an 18-page list of offences ranging from murder and child neglect to 'living off the earnings of male prostitution' or 'lewd, indecent or libidinous behaviour'.[52] Therefore, these offences range from convictions for very serious offences for which somebody would be imprisoned for many years, to cautions for less serious offences. They also include offences which may have no bearing on somebody's fitness to work in a particular role.

Second, the 'barring decision-making process' is a series of stages (involving the application of 'tools' and 'tests') through which caseworkers progress in order to decide whether to bar somebody or not. These caseworkers are not in general experts in sex offences or the professions and do not meet the person they are considering barring. Instead, they apply systematic procedures to the information with which they have been presented. One of these tools is the 'structured judgement process' (SJP), 'an internal risk assessment tool developed to help determine whether… there is a future risk of harm to vulnerable groups'.[53] This involves the caseworker allotting risk weightings 1-5 to various factors which may make someone a risk to children: these include 'poor problem solving/coping skills', 'irresponsible and reckless', 'impulsive, chaotic and impulsive lifestyle', 'poor intimacy skills' and 'excessive/obsessive interest in sex'.[54]

The Home Office claims that both the autobar and the SJP represent an attempt to make decisions 'in relation to standardised points of reference that minimise subjective decision-making'.[55] Yet both have come under substantial challenge, both for their scientific basis and procedural fairness.

The Royal College of Nursing (RCN) has successfully challenged auto-barring decisions on behalf of its members. In October 2010, the organisation won a judicial review on behalf of several claimants who had received autobars. One nurse had received a caution for child neglect, after his wife – unbeknownst to him – had left their children alone for a short time while he was at work. Another claimant was a nurse who had left her 11-year old at home alone for a short period while she went shopping, and received a similar caution (the Nursing and Midwifery Council had reviewed her case but decided that there was no case to answer).[56]

Meanwhile, the Structured Judgement Procedure (responsible for 'discretionary bars') has been questioned by social work professionals and sex offender experts. In the view of social work professor Eileen Munro, the procedure appeared to be based on 'very subjective judgements'. She asks: 'What is a "suspicious/angry style of relating to others"?' She questioned whether there had been 'any testing of the reliability or validity of this decision-making. If this were a drug, the Committee on the Safety of Medicines would insist on doing very robust trials to see whether it was having any of its claimed effects.'[57]

Similarly, child protection consultant Paul Roffey criticises the 'strong bureaucratic element in the barring system', and the focus on 'ensuring that everything is done in a certain way'. He also criticised the fact that caseworkers made a barring decision without meeting the person concerned, and that these caseworkers were not generally experts in sex offences or the relevant professions. 'Meeting the person is absolutely essential', he argues, 'you need to do your own assessment. And you need to be someone who is experienced in this area, otherwise you could be naïve or risk averse.'[58]

Some of these discretionary bars are the result of reports sent to the ISA/DBS, as part of the new 'duty to refer', under which organisations must report people for behaviour that they believe has harmed or may harm a child or other vulnerable person (the definition of 'harm' is broad, including 'emotional/ psychological harm' such as 'inflexible regimes and lack of choice').[59] As a result, the ISA/DBS receives reports of incidents which have not been tested in a court or administrative tribunal, meaning that the reported incident could be misrepresented, or even invented. An individual could be barred who had never been prosecuted for or convicted of an offence, or had any contact with the police or a professional tribunal. There were 13,000 'referrals for barring' in the first two years of the ISA.[60] In one case, a priest was referred to the ISA by his diocesan safeguarding officer for refusing to undergo a CRB check; evidence submitted to the ISA included derisory comments about safety signs he had made in the church newsletter.[61]

In this respect, the current barring system is inferior to a court hearing, or a professional tribunal, which could decide to convict somebody of an offence or bar them from a profession. The barring decision is made by non-expert caseworkers applying formal procedures of questionable scientific value, without meeting the person concerned.

The primary result of this barring process has been the widening of the net and the barring of a greater number of people. Since the ISA took over barring from the Department for Education, the barred list has increased from around 16,000 to 50,000.[62] As a result, it becomes more difficult to establish whether somebody poses a risk to children, since the barred list includes people who received minor cautions and those who have committed unrelated professional failings together with serious offenders, some of whom are child sex abusers. Tellingly, the DBS was unable to answer the question of how many child sex offenders there are.[63]

Part of the problem is that the barred lists are performing several different functions. In part, the DBS barred list duplicates the role of a professional body's barred list, which would result from a decision made by an independent tribunal after some failing in professional practice (which may or may not be a criminal offence). The DBS barred list also includes people convicted of sex offences – therefore doubling the role of the Sex Offenders' Register – as well as people convicted or cautioned for other serious offences.

Rosalind Hooper, Royal College of Nursing senior legal officer, argues that the 'vulnerable adults' barred list is in some ways a rough tool with 'too heavy a clout'. Somebody barred from nursing, for example, could be quite suitable for other healthcare positions: 'a nurse could be inadequate at medication, but she could be an excellent healthcare assistant'. Yet a person barred from work or volunteering with 'vulnerable adults' would be prevented from volunteering at the local homeless charity, or working in another caring profession. This problem is accentuated for professions such as healthcare assistants, which lack their own professional bodies and are only regulated by the DBS.

Therefore, if the policy goal is to prevent child sex offenders from working with children, then both the barring and the criminal records system appear to be rough and inadequate means to achieve this objective.

# 4

# A Different Approach

The criminal records check has become so engrained in our culture that it is hard to imagine a society in which they do not exist on their present scale. Yet it is important to remember that the UK's vetting and barring system is not an average and reasonable child protection measure: instead, it is an historical and international exception. There is no other country which has a system on this scale, with the objective of checking all those who have a certain kind of contact with children in the public sphere.

An extensive survey of criminal records policies in the *European Journal of Probation* found that, in general, other European countries have a system whereby individuals can apply for an extract of their criminal records when applying for particular jobs.[64] This only shows convictions for longer periods of imprisonment and is largely for use in relation to occupations such as banks, private security companies and state or administration employees (including those working with children). Germany has a system of enhanced criminal records checks (the 'erweiterte Führungszeugnis'), which applies to child professionals such as nursery school teachers or social workers, but not largely to volunteers. That is, criminal records checks play the same approximate role as in the UK prior to 2002.

Only in some Australian states has there been a systematic checking of volunteers who work with children. Under the State of Victoria's Working with Children Act 2005, for example, there is a legal requirement to check all adults who have 'direct contact' with children through work or volunteering.[65] However, even these Australian policies appear relaxed by British standards. The state of Victoria, for example, excludes many groups from vetting requirements, including parent volunteers, some student volunteers, workers from another Australian state, teachers, and police officers.[66]

Therefore, the first step in rethinking the vetting and barring system is to recognise that this is not the only approach to child protection; in fact, on the contrary, it is highly unusual. If one starts from the social policy goal of preventing sex offenders from having access to children, or identifying those who present a risk to children, the national vetting and barring system is not necessarily the best means of achieving this objective.

The first point to recognise is that convicted child sex offenders represent a very small minority of the general population. That is, there are substantially fewer than 50,000 individuals[67] with some form of child sex offence, yet there are several million people who work or volunteer with children or 'vulnerable adults'. The current policy focuses on the several million people: everyone must obtain clearance before they come into contact with children. But this means, essentially, that most of the time and effort is expended on checking people who pose no risk at all, including mothers and grandmothers listening to reading in school. It would make more sense to concentrate on mechanisms that target the small number of known sex offenders. This would also be a better method of achieving the deterrent effect which some claim for criminal records checks.

More targeted mechanisms would include, for example, tightening up and increasing investment in the probation system, or the police systems for visiting sex offenders upon release from prison. At the current time, the opposite is occurring: the government recently privatised a large portion of the probation system, with 160,000 offenders now being supervised by community rehabilitation companies, in spite of warnings from the Commons Public Accounts Committee about potential risks to public safety.[68]

In addition to probation services, police forces have a responsibility to visit sex offenders living in their communities, but these departments are not in general well funded, and indeed this probation-type role is out of key with the normal police work of gaining convictions. Former chief constable Julie Spence says that in general this is the responsibility of a 'small team' which is an 'adjunct to the child protection team; they don't have an enormous budget'. She argues that many forces do not have the resources or manpower to deal with such probation supervision as extensively as people may think: 'the most risky individuals could get visits weekly or a couple of times a month, and the least risky would be far less, perhaps once every few months'.[69]

Another possible avenue of social policy focus would be improving police child protection departments, focusing on investigating abuse allegations or concerns, and ensuring convictions in cases where abuse can be proven. Julie Spence notes that many police child protection departments are the poor cousin of criminal investigation, indeed historically one of the worst funded departments. She reports that when she ran

Cambridgeshire Police the force was 'spending far more on the team doing the CRB checks, because they were specifically funded by government, than we were actually putting into child protection. In most forces, more money goes into checks than into investigation.' Therefore, police forces are spending more time running database searches on low- or no-risk individuals than on investigating allegations or reports of abuse. Clearly, this is not the most rational allocation of time or money.

The criminal records check system is based on large amounts of information exchange and release about a large number of individuals. This means ample opportunities for incorrect or irrelevant information to damage people's careers; it also means an inherent lack of discernment and judgement about which pieces of information are relevant and which are not. The DBS now plays the role of judging authority, but without the rigour or protections of a legal process. This raises the risk of people being unfairly barred; it also raises the risk that serious incidents are not picked up, because an apparently minor incident was not properly investigated. In establishing guilt or innocence, there is no replacement for proper police investigation and court trial, where evidence can be pursued and tested. It is notable that many of the shocking cases of child abuse in recent years – from Jimmy Savile to the Catholic church – involved individuals without criminal records: the failure was a failure to report and to investigate allegations, rather than a lack of checking.

Therefore, a more rational allocation of time and money would focus child protection on known and suspected individuals who present a risk to children, through probation and police investigation – rather than on the general population.

Finally, we must mention the importance of informal vigilance for ensuring the safety of children. This means children being able and willing to report instances of abuse or suspicious behaviour to other adults, for which it is important that they have a number of trusted adults to whom they can turn. It also means adults in an organisation keeping a look out for children and following up instances of suspicious behaviour. Adults who work or volunteer with children are not doing so in a vacuum: they are in a club or organisation where there are other adults around or working directly with them. Children talk both to their parents and to other adults about their experiences.

Shaun Joynson, a volunteer with the Scouts and other youth organisations for 35 years, says that he has seen little positive role for criminal records checks in preventing abuse or potential abuse. Instead, the most powerful child protection mechanism that he has witnessed is informal vigilance: children talking to other adults about incidents, which were then picked up on. He gives several examples of how, over the years, he has encountered people whose behaviour 'rung alarm bells': in every case the person had clean criminal records, yet their behaviour with children was suspicious and quite different to that of other adults. He and others picked up on these signs and removed these individuals from the Scout group.[70]

Similarly, Carrie Herbert, founder and president of the children's charity Red Balloon, says that in her experience checks are of limited value. In the cases of sexual harassment of children she has encountered through her work, the perpetrators all had clean criminal records. She concludes that 'if checks were abolished, it wouldn't have made an iota of difference – I see them as a complete waste of time.'[71]

Professor Eileen Munro argues that these informal protection systems are more important than official systems, and can be weakened by the over-reliance on formal procedures such as criminal records checks: 'Official systems play such a small part in human safety. It's a bad idea to let the general public feel that safety is somebody else's business – and that is one of the adverse consequences of having such a high profile vetting and barring service.'

She points to the importance of people using their intuition and being proactive when they encounter others who are behaving suspiciously. 'If an employer has concerns about a member of staff, they should seek to monitor them, to see if their concerns are validated at all. If you are a parent, you don't do a CRB check when you are worried about someone: you don't let your child near them again.'

At this point, we should recall the warnings of the Home Office research on criminal records in the early 1990s, which argued that criminal records checks could give a 'false sense of security' and weaken systems of informal vigilance. There is no substantial research into whether or not this is the case. However, there have been cases of child abuse – such as that of nursery worker Vanessa George – where fellow staff failed to act upon or challenge suspicious behaviour. There are also reports from volunteering organisations that people who have clean checks are seen as having 'passed the test'[72], and cannot be questioned. It is certainly logical that when child protection becomes primarily a matter of 'box ticking', and criminal records checks become the index of trustworthiness, people would rely less on their judgement and be less willing to take the initiative when they encounter suspicious behaviour.

# Conclusion:
# Criminal Records Checks in
# Perspective

The rise of mass criminal records checks was not driven by social policy, because of the effectiveness of these procedures in preventing child abuse. On the contrary, the policy assessments of vetting in the early 1990s highlighted the ineffective nature and negative side-effects of criminal records checks, and recommended that they be limited.

The expansion of vetting in the 1990s and early 2000s was driven not by social policy but by institutions, as an increasingly fearful culture fuelled a demand for checks from organisations, and checks fast acquired the status of a seal of approval for childcare workers ('despite their deficiencies', as the 1993 Home Office consultation observed).[73]

The development of the vetting and barring scheme in the wake of Ian Huntley's murders in 2002 reversed this relationship between policy and culture. Now, rather than policy attempting to put a break on a fearful culture, policy was going further than culture, demanding state vetting as a legal obligation. However, this was not a rational response to the Huntley case: it is an obvious irony that the new vetting system would not have stopped the single case it was set up to prevent, since Ian Huntley did not work at the school of the girls he murdered, and they had come to his house that day not to see him but to see his partner.

After the state attempted to define the category of 'regulated activity', ideas that had been latent in culture and expressed erratically, depending on the context, became formalised as a legal obligation. The category of 'regulated activity' enshrined in law the assumption that encounters between adults and children are inherently risky, and that vetting and other forms of state monitoring are the index of trustworthiness.

In spite of certain changes, this basic assumption remains the fulcrum of the current government's vetting and barring policy. The regulation of 'relationships of trust' continues apace, with the consequent illogicality, expense, and obstruction to social life. Indeed, the current fragmented system of repeat criminal records checks is perhaps even more obstructive than the vetting database would have been; it is certainly more expensive.

Policy now leads culture in the spreading of fear; it makes mistrust a legal obligation, subject to criminal sanction. Mass vetting means the propagation of suspicion as a default bearing towards others, and the concomitant default faith placed in bureaucratic checks as indicating a person's respectability and character. Both common sense and professional judgement are bypassed in favour of databases and standardised procedures.

Vetting is still the key element of child protection policy, but the primary cited source for its efficacy – the Mori survey for the CRB/DBS – shows that the 'unsuitable people' losing jobs because of criminal records checks are not child sex offenders. This is a system for which the costs and negative side-effects are all too clear, while significant positive effects have yet to be revealed.

Over four years after the reforms of the vetting and barring system, it is clear that they have failed to achieve their primary objectives. Vetting has not been 'scaled back' and people have not started to 'trust one another again'. A key reason for this failure was that the reforms left intact the essential basis of the Safeguarding Vulnerable Groups Act, retaining the obligatory vetting of 'relationships of trust' between children and adults.

Four years ago, some of those companies making money from criminal records checks may have worried for their margins, but now they can rest assured. As Tata Consultancy begins to overhaul the vetting and barring computer system, the next phase of the scheme begins, creating the potential for criminal records checks to be further extended into people's everyday lives.

In subjecting this vetting and barring system to scrutiny, this report emphasises that the problems that prompted the reforms four years ago have not been solved. First and foremost, this is a call for social policy research and public debate on the subject, in the hope that future reforms may have somewhat more success in 'scaling back' this unique and labyrinthine system.

# NOTES

1.   http://www.theguardian.com/politics/2010/jun/15/child-worker-vetting-scheme-review
2.   http://www.telegraph.co.uk/culture/books/booknews/5834646/Philip-Pullman-refuses-to-undergo-insulting-child-safety-check.html
3.   http://www.capitallaw.co.uk/site/publicationsandnews/publicationsandfactsheets/newsbytes/employment_newsbytes/employment5jan13.html
4.   Figure cited in the House of Lords debate, Column 914: http://www.publications.parliament.uk/pa/ld201212/ldhansrd/text/120321-0001.htm
   Also, the impact assessment: https://www.gov.uk/government/uploads/system/uploads/attachment_data/file/98414/changes-vb-cr-regime-ia.pdf
5.   FOI response from the DBS, 12 May 2014
6.   Email from Scout volunteer, 4 February 2014
7.   FOI response from the DBS, 21 March 2014. The data included the period from 1 April 2013 until 6 March 2014.
8.   Interview, Shaun Joynson, 27 March 2014. The local authorities' claim goes against current guidance which states that volunteers should only be checked if they are in sole charge of children.
9.   https://www.gov.uk/government/uploads/system/uploads/attachment_data/file/223723/DBS_Annual_Report_V1_0.pdf – DBS annual report and accounts, 1 December 2012 to 31 March 2013
10.   List of all umbrella and registered bodies from DBS FOI response, 24 June 2013
11.   ISA, report and accounts, April 2012-Nov 2012
12.   Quoted in Regulating Trust: who will be on the vetting database? Manifesto Club briefing document http://www.manifestoclub.com/files/RegulatingTrust.pdf
13.   Draft Guidance for the Vetting and Barring Scheme, Home Office, May 2009
14.   Drawing the Line, Roger Singleton, December 2009 http://webarchive.nationalarchives.gov.uk/20130401151715/http://www.education.gov.uk/publications/eOrderingDownload/DCSF-01122-2009.pdf
15.   https://www.gov.uk/government/uploads/system/uploads/attachment_data/file/97875/leaflet-england-wales.pdf Received royal assent in May 2012

[16] Guidance on the meaning of 'supervision'
http://media.education.gov.uk/assets/files/pdf/s/supervision%20guidance%20revised%20sos%20sept%202012.pdf

[17] Guidance on the meaning of 'supervision'
http://media.education.gov.uk/assets/files/pdf/r/regulated%20activity%20children%20full%20information%20ewni%20final%202012-06-01.pdf

[18] Guidance on the meaning of 'supervision'
http://media.education.gov.uk/assets/files/pdf/s/supervision%20guidance%20revised%20sos%20sept%202012.pdf

[19] See the Volunteering England guide to 'regulated activity'
http://www.volunteering.org.uk/images/stories/Volunteering-England/Documents/Free-Information-Sheets/ra%20children%20and%20young%20people%20flowchart%20v2.pdf

[20] Discussion on mumsnet: http://www.mumsnet.com/Talk/primary/a1413593-CRBs-for-parent-volunteers-what-does-your-school-do

[21] Discussion on mumsnet: http://www.mumsnet.com/Talk/primary/a1413593-CRBs-for-parent-volunteers-what-does-your-school-do

[22] For example, in Don't Touch!: The Educational Story of a Panic, Heather Piper & Ian Stronach, Routledge, 2008, p.30

[23] Joanne M Smith, 'Prior Criminality and Employment of Social Workers', Br J Social Wk (1999) 29, 49-68

[24] Q&A: Vetting school staff, BBC News, 18 December 2003;
http://news.bbc.co.uk/2/hi/uk_news/education/3331121.stm

[25] Sellers of explosives are required only to have standard security check; a Saturday cricket coach must have enhanced clearance. Volunteers are very conscious that they are subject to the formal requirements of a job, but they lack the corresponding rights: they have no rights to a hearing or union representation in the case of an accusation, for example. As such, people who require a clean criminal records check for their work sometimes avoid volunteering.

[26] 'Safeguarding Children and Safer Recruitment',
https://www.gov.uk/government/publications/safeguarding-children-and-safer-recruitment

[27] Email to Manifesto Club, March 2012; and
http://www.manifestoclub.com/node/903

[28] https://www.gov.uk/government/uploads/system/uploads/attachment_data/file/269386/Update_Service_Applicant_guide_v3.8.pdf

[29]  Including: £44 fee for enhanced DBS check; £20 administration
fee; £13 update service

[30]  https://www.gov.uk/disclosure-and-barring-service-criminal-
record-checks-referrals-and-complaints

[31]  http://www.criminalrecordsagency.co.uk/News.aspx

[32]  https://www.gov.uk/government/uploads/system/uploads/
attachment_data/file/269386/Update_Service_Applicant_guide
_v3.8.pdf

[33]  http://www.moneycontrol.com/news/business/tcs-bags-8-
year-contractuk-govt-for-350m-pounds_765472.html

[34]  TCS is responsible for overhauling the computer system for
criminal records checks, making them faster, online and
improving 'information exchange' between the disclosure and
barring parts of the service.
http://www.tcs.com/news_events/press_releases/Pages/TCS_
multi-million_pound_contract_UK_Home_Office.aspx

[35]  FOI response from the DBS, 24 June 2013

[36]  On the basis that the company would charge an average
administration fee of £20 per check

[37]  DBS – Corporate Plan, 2013 / 2014
https://www.gov.uk/government/uploads/system/uploads/at
tachment_data/file/204582/DBS_Corporate_Plan_2013_2014.pdf

[38]  FOI response from the DBS, 04 February 2013. A similar figure is
frequently quoted to the press and in publicity.

[39]  The 2012 Mori report found a small number of people who have
lost jobs because of sex offences, but not child sex offences. The
2009 and 2011 reports did not mention sex offences, suggesting
that these were either non-existent or so few as to not be worth
mentioning.

[40]  Email to Josie Appleton, 9 January 2014

[41]  'Voluntary Action Research, Second Series, Paper no. 2, Criminal
checks within the voluntary sector, an evaluation of the pilot
schemes', by Judith Unell, The Volunteer Centre UK (evaluation
commissioned by the Home Office), 1992

[42]  Voluntary Action Research, Second Series, Paper no. 2, 'Criminal
checks within the voluntary sector, an evaluation of the pilot
schemes', by Judith Unell, The Volunteer Centre UK (evaluation
commissioned by the Home Office) 1992, pp.12, 112 &21

[43]  *Ibid*, p.105

[44]  *Ibid*, p.104

[45]  'Disclosure of Criminal Records for Employment Vetting
Purposes', A consultation paper by the Home Office, September
1993

46 Disclosure of Criminal Records for Employment Vetting Purposes', A consultation paper by the Home Office, September 1993, p8-9. The pilot study report also made this point: 'checking is concentrated on that half of the population which is relatively unlikely to offend and extremely unlikely to offend sexually.' 'Criminal checks within the voluntary sector, an evaluation of the pilot schemes', Judith Unell, p. 29

47 'Disclosure of Criminal Records for Employment Vetting Purposes', A consultation paper by the Home Office, September 1993, p.9

48 Disclosure of Criminal Records for Employment Vetting Purposes', A consultation paper by the Home Office, September 1993, p.29

49 Interview with Christopher Stacey, March 2014

50 'Criminal checks within the voluntary sector, an evaluation of the pilot schemes', Judith Unell, p.70

51 The Department of Education had held a 'list 99', people barred from the teaching profession; this became 'list under Section 142 of the Education Act 2002'. Two additional lists were created in 1999-2000: the Protection of Children act 1999 List, held by the Department for Education, included the barring of social workers, and those who worked in child care homes and nurseries; and the 'Protection of Vulnerable Adults list', held by the Department of Health, made under the Care Standards Act 2000, which was a list of those barred from the adult social care sector or other caring professions such as nursing.

52 https://www.gov.uk/government/uploads/system/uploads/attachment_data/file/249429/dbs-factsheet-relevant-offences.pdf

53 https://www.gov.uk/government/uploads/system/uploads/attachment_data/file/249427/dbs-factsheet-referral-and-barring-decision-making-process.pdf

54 https://www.gov.uk/government/uploads/system/uploads/attachment_data/file/227649/dbs-barring-decision-process-sjp-template.pdf

55 Draft Guidance for the Vetting and Barring Scheme, Home Office, May 2009

56 http://www.rcn.org.uk/newsevents/press_releases/uk/rcn_judicial_review_on_vetting_and_barring_scheme

57 Interview with Eileen Munro, February 2014

58 Interview, January 2014

59 DBS factsheet: https://www.gov.uk/government/uploads/system/uploads/attachment_data/file/249422/dbs-factsheet-harm-relevant-conduct-and-risk-of-harm.pdf

60 http://www.telegraph.co.uk/news/uknews/law-and-order/9250256/Thousands-reported-to-vetting-agency-but-only-4-barred.html
61 Case file from Jeremy Hummerstone; submission to the ISA made by the Devon diocese safeguarding officer.
62 The ISA inherited barred lists of 16,365 (see: ISA Freedom of Information Response, July 2010 https://www.whatdotheyknow.com/request/number_of_barrings_by_the_isa#incoming-103774). There were 49,704 individuals on the children's barred list in June 2013. The majority – 32,780 – were as a result of an autobar. (Statistics obtained from DBS FOI response, 24 June 2013)
63 In response to a Freedom of Information Request, it said that it could only obtain this information through case-by-case analysis.
64 *European Journal of Probation*, vol. 3, no 1, 2011
65 For example, see the Working With Children Act 2005 in the state of Victoria http://www.legislation.vic.gov.au/domino/Web_Notes/LDMS/LTObject_Store/LTObjSt5.nsf/d1a8d8a9bed958efca25761600042ef5/fe6e82192f34c57fca25778a00179e36/$FILE/05-57a027.pdf
66 http://www.workingwithchildren.vic.gov.au/home/about+the+check/who+needs+a+check/exemptions/exemptions
67 On the basis that there are 50,000 people of the children's barred list, but that this includes a broad range of individuals many of whom are not child sex offenders.
68 http://www.theguardian.com/society/2014/may/20/mps-warn-probation-service-privatisation
69 Interview with Julie Spence
70 Interview with Shaun Joynson, March 2014
71 Interview with Carrie Herbert, February 2014
72 Interview with a volunteer for an elderly people's charity, January 2014
73 'Disclosure of Criminal Records for Employment Vetting Purposes', A consultation paper by the Home Office, September 1993, p.29